Senior Year Step-by-Step

Simple Instructions for Busy Homeschool Parents

Lee Binz,
The HomeScholar

First Printing, 2014

Printed in the United States of America

Cover Design by Robin Montoya
Edited by Kimberly Charron

ISBN: 1503155838
ISBN-13: 978-1503155831

Senior Year Step-by-Step

Simple Instructions for Busy Homeschool Parents

What are Coffee Break Books?

Senior Year Step-by-Step is part of The HomeScholar's Coffee Break Book series.

This series is designed especially for parents who don't want to spend hours and hours reading a 400-page book on homeschooling high school. Each book combines Lee's practical and friendly approach with detailed, but easy-to-digest information. They are perfect to read over a cup of coffee at your favorite coffee shop!

Never overwhelming, always accessible and manageable, each book in the series will give parents the tools they need to tackle the tasks of homeschooling high school, one warm sip at a time.

Everything about these Coffee Break Books is designed to suggest simplicity, ease, and comfort—from the size (fits in a purse), to the font and paragraph length (easy on the eyes), to the price (the same as a Starbucks Venti Triple Caramel Macchiato). Unlike a fancy coffee drink, however, these books are guilt-free pleasures you will want to enjoy again and again!

Table of Contents

Introduction

Transitions and Goals

Seasons of Transition

There are four seasons of homeschooling: caretaker, teacher, mentor, and friend. At first, you're primarily the caretaker and love-giver. You have a babe in arms who, with your nurturing, grows into a toddler. As you move into the elementary years, your role as teacher becomes more prominent. You start to teach your child how to read, write, and do math. Toward middle school and high school, you get to the point where you're much more of a mentor or guide than you are a teacher. This transition between the teacher role and the mentor role often makes parents insecure.

The final transition is from primarily a mentor to more of a friend. During senior year, you will start that transition from mentor to friend. Looking back on the homeschool years, the role of friend to my children promises to be the longest and the sweetest season of all.

Senior year is a time of transition. Think about those changes you experienced when you had a baby. Your newborn was different from your four-year-old. Likewise, your high school freshman will be different from your high school senior. Finally, your confident and mature high school graduate will be a different person when they graduate college. Four years can make a big difference in maturity.

Consider Your Goals

As your child starts their senior year, think about your goals. You want to launch your child successfully into the world. Often, this means admission into college—either a four-year university or community college. You also want them to have meaningful employment.

Ultimately, your child must support themselves and their future family, pay for their own living situation, their own car, and their own gas money.

Remember that teenagers change their minds. One day, they may want a job as an auto mechanic, and the next they may want to be a mechanical engineer.

Plan for college admission and scholarships so you are prepared. Should the end of senior year come around and your child suddenly decides to be an engineer, a doctor, a lawyer, a teacher or any other profession requiring a college degree, you will still have a plan in place.

Chapter 1

Summer Before Senior Year

Evaluate Your Situation

The first day of senior year is when you will start filling out applications. During the summer prior, look over colleges where your student will apply. Evaluate your situation and determine what your child has accomplished and what they still need to do.

Are there classes your child still needs for university admission? You have plenty of time—a whole year. If they are missing economics or art, you have all of senior year to fill in the gaps.

Are there any tests your child needs to take? Perhaps one of the colleges where your child plans to apply requires SAT subject tests or a certain number of AP exams. By looking at your situation the summer before 12th grade, you can plan to meet individual college requirements.

Update Your Records

During the summer before senior year, make sure your homeschool records are up to date. Your child's transcript and course descriptions should be completely ready to send to colleges.

Creating a transcript is extremely important. You don't want to be *that* parent who forgets to include something important on the official high school record! You don't want to be *that* parent who puts it off and becomes the weakest link, so your child misses out on college admission and scholarships.

You may be wondering why transcripts are important. In 12th grade, you need the transcript to complete your homeschool records that colleges will want to see. But even beyond 12th grade, your transcript remains important. Your homeschool transcript may be used later on, after your child enters the work force, when an employer wants to see this record. It may become important after college, when your child wants to attend graduate school or land a special job. Just because your child doesn't need a transcript today, doesn't mean they will never need the transcript.

I encourage all parents who homeschool high school to complete a high school transcript, and keep it safe forever. As the school of record, it's our job to preserve these important records. You may need a transcript even if...

- your child is joining the military
- your child is attending community college
- your child is completing college credits by exam
- your child is enrolled in an online degree program
- your child was accepted into college without a homeschool transcript

- your child has an advanced degree after college

Life is funny, and strange and unexpected things can happen. Even if you don't think you need a transcript right now, your child may still need one later on for graduate school or employment. Every year I get calls from panicky parents desperate to complete their transcripts and course descriptions for their adult children. It may seem a daunting task this summer, but believe me it's easier to do it now than it will be five or ten years from now! So please, *please*, make a homeschool transcript for your children! No matter what, don't skip this important responsibility of homeschool parents! Be ready.

Colleges go through a lengthy and arduous process looking over students to admit. They typically have only a couple of minutes to make a thumbs-up or thumbs-down decision on an applicant. For this reason, the transcript might be the only section of information they utilize for determination. It's a single, one-page summary of the student that conveys essential information.

Is the student qualified? Do they satisfy the minimum requirements? The less difficult the transcript is to decipher, the more they will desire to pay attention to information regarding your child.

Along with the transcript, be ready to provide a comprehensive record. Are your high school records organized in a neat, easily digestible format that colleges will understand and appreciate?

Comprehensive records can include:

- Transcript
- Course descriptions
- Reading list
- Awards and activity list
- Samples of work

There are a few situations in particular when course descriptions can be extremely important:

1. When applying to a very selective college.

2. When parents can't afford the full cost of college without scholarship money.
3. When your college asks for, prefers, or requires course information.
4. When the child wants to go to only one particular college.

In each of these situations, providing detailed homeschool records can significantly improve your child's chances of earning college admission and scholarships.

It's difficult, although not impossible, to pull together records for the entire four years of high school during the summer before senior year, or worse yet, during the first few weeks of senior year. Parents in this situation can feel overwhelmed to the point of being immobilized. The easy way is to ensure you update all your homeschool records every spring, so they're always ready to go.

If you need help, I have great resources for both transcripts and course descriptions available at:

www.TotalTranscriptSolution.com and
www.ComprehensiveRecordSolution.com

Prepare for the National Merit Scholarship

If your child tends to score well on standardized tests (in the 90th percentile), you may hear back about the National Merit Scholarship at the end of summer after your child takes the PSAT in 11th grade. Records are especially important if you have a child who may qualify for the National Merit Scholarship. Completed records are extremely helpful for filling out all the paperwork involved!

As a homeschool parent, you are the school and have to fill out the paperwork. For the National Merit Scholarship, you don't want to be the weakest link, so make sure your child's records are ready. Students are notified about their level of scholarship (Commended Student or Semifinalist) in September. This quick turn-around time can make life difficult if you don't already have information prepared and organized. In October, parents will need to submit a very detailed application. In November, you need to send SAT scores to the National Merit Scholarship Corporation. Make sure if your child missed the SAT in junior year, they take it first thing in senior year.

In March of senior year, Finalists will be notified. Monetary awards are given out later in the spring.

Collect College Information

You should have already chosen some colleges to apply to with your child. Make sure these colleges include a reach, a fit, and a safety school.

A "reach" school means your child meets all requirements but their test scores don't quite measure up. It would be unusual if the college admitted your child but you're going to give it a try. Ivy League schools and military academies are always reach schools no matter how smart and well-rounded your child.

A "fit" school is one for which your child meets all requirements and expectations and their SAT or ACT score is a perfect fit. There's a high likelihood they will gain admission to a fit school.

A "safety" school is one for which your child exceeds requirements and has better scores than most of the students who apply. They are almost certain to get into a safety school. Safety schools are just in case all the other schools say "no." They are your backup plan for a place your child can attend in the fall.

During this information collection phase before senior year starts, request applications and put deadlines on the calendar. You can request a fee waiver, particularly if you have visited the college. Each application can cost $50 or more. Avoid paying the fee by simply asking for a fee waiver on your campus visit.

Remember to apply well in advance of the deadline. It's like dealing with the federal government—you don't want to mess up those deadlines. The due dates may also be much earlier than expected, so closely watch all deadlines. Missing one deadline may eliminate the chance of scholarships.

One of my Gold Care Club members applied to a school with an early decision in July or August. This is a little detail you want to know well before September! Collecting this information in the summer before senior year will help.

Read the details on each application from each school. Every college you apply to is unique and will each have their own criteria. You do not want to be surprised by the fine print.

Summer Activities for Teens

During this final summer of high school, seek meaningful activities for your teen. You want some activities that will look good on your child's activity list. Include activities displaying leadership skills. For example, they might teach a chess class or work at a summer camp. Your child can do some volunteer work or gain valuable employment experience, whether or not it's in the field they are considering as a career.

All of these activities show socialization skills and character. They can demonstrate self-motivation, which is important because colleges don't always assume homeschoolers have great social skills!

Make sure your child reads books over the summer. They don't have to be "great books," simply encourage your child to choose some books to read. These books can be added to the reading list you submit to colleges.

My children found the books they read from college-bound reading lists were often studied in college as well. This gave them a bit of an edge. You can find a great college-bound reading list on my site:

HomeHighSchoolHelp.com/college-bound-reading-list

For more summer activities, consider having your child take CLEP tests for dual credit. First, find out whether earning college credit through CLEP tests would be of benefit to the colleges where your child is applying. Some colleges accept credits earned through CLEP, and some don't.

You might consider starting to work on college applications during the summer, especially if your fall schedule tends to be busy. This might be something to consider if your child is taking dual credit courses at a community college in the fall. If you know this will be the case, you may want to start on applications in the summer.

Remember, as teenagers get older, we as parents get to the stage when we can't always tell them what to do. We start moving towards the friend stage and sometimes teenagers are not very cooperative. When my son was 2 years old, he would sometimes get tired and sit on the grocery store floor refusing to move. When senior year comes around, our children can have moments like this, too. That's one of the reasons I recommend practicing on applications during junior year, in case your child flat out refuses to in senior year – at least they did some work in junior year they can submit!

Chapter 2

Fall of Senior Year

On the first day of senior year, start working on college applications together. Spend at least an hour a day working on them. Some applications will be handled directly through the college itself, and some will be filled out through the common application.

Admission deadlines vary. Most advisors, especially financial advisors, recommend you complete applications well before Thanksgiving. The first ones in line for college will often get the scholarships. Getting done early can pay off in real scholarship money!

Records, Forms, and Deadlines

Fall of senior year will be filled with forms – they will blur in front of you after a while! There are application essays – each college may have as many as four essays your child will be required to write. Then there are letters of recommendation—you have to make sure they are each completed and turned into the college on time. You also want to make sure you've submitted test scores to the right place at the right time (with the right scores).

Make sure your transcript is ready to go in the fall. You'll also need to have course descriptions complete. Many colleges will ask for them, and good course descriptions may earn your child more scholarship money! If you need help creating course descriptions (they can be very time-consuming), check out my Comprehensive Record Solution at www.ComprehensiveRecordSolution.com

One mother told me about the hours she spent perfecting her course descriptions. Then she shared her child's huge scholarship award. This real homeschool mom calculated that her work on comprehensive records *paid* her—time consuming of course, but it may pay off in a big way.

Your child's reading list and activity list need to be ready. Watch for anything supplemental the college might want, such as a homeschool description or your homeschool philosophy. Give colleges anything they request.

Write Application Essays

Application essays can be intimidating. They have to be perfectly written, entertaining, compelling, and memorable. These are technically perfect, self-reflective essays. That was always a struggle for us because I have two boys and teenage boys are not always naturally self-reflective!

Essays often need to be 500 to 1,000 words or longer, which can seem very long to teens. There may be 1 to 4 application essays required per college. However, most colleges ask for similar topics, so your child may not have to write as many essays as you might think.

Collect essay topics from all the colleges where your child is applying, and then brainstorm together. Sometimes we as parents may remember something about their life that our child has forgotten or vice versa. By brainstorming together, you might be able to remind your child about events they can write about in their essays. Scrapbooks and photo albums can be helpful for remembering significant events from the past.

Never repeat anything between essays going to the same college. For example, I only allowed my child who loves chess to use the word "chess" in one essay per college. My other child, who loves economics and history, was only allowed to mention "economics" or "Thomas Jefferson" in one of his college application essays. Make sure no subjects are repeated from essay to essay.

Think about each application essay as a word picture. Each essay is like a portrait the child is creating of themselves. Each needs to be taken from a different perspective - each self-portrait describes a different facet of your child's life.

You can modify the essays and use them again, over and over between colleges. Have your child take one essay and change a few words so it is specific to each of the different colleges being applied to. This makes for less work.

Make sure each essay is edited to perfection. Not only should a parent look over each one, but also somebody outside the family. Notice, I said "edited," not "re-written." This is important to remember. Always do a final spell-check. Although it won't pick up everything, you will be amazed at the little things you can catch with a spell-check.

Send Homeschool Records

Fall is the time to send out transcripts and records to colleges. It is okay to send your child's college application separately from homeschool records—they don't have to be sent at the same time. Think about how it's done by the public schools—the child fills out the application forms and turns them in, and the school fills out the school information and turns that in. They're not mailed at the same time. It does save money on postage if you mail everything together at once. But if you need to, for time's sake, you can submit the information separately.

Even if your transcript looks great on paper, it can be confusing to figure out how to submit a homeschool transcript when you are filling out college applications during the fall of senior year. Let me give you a few quick tips.

Classes

Include all the classes your child is currently taking on the transcript. Are you beginning chemistry or calculus this fall? Put it on the high school transcript. If your child intends to take certain classes in community college, include the names of these classes. Colleges expect this, and assume it is just an "estimate" of what the child will be taking.

Grades

Don't include final grades for classes you haven't completed yet. Instead, indicate grades are in progress (IP) or yet to be determined (TBD). Define whichever term you use at the bottom of the transcript. You can indicate how many credits they will be earning, but don't put a grade for a class until the grade is assigned.

Transcripts

When you are submitting a transcript in the fall, it's simply a "transcript." You may need to send in a transcript after first semester, an "interim transcript" that includes grades earned through December. Finally, when school is over for the year, you will be asked to submit a "final transcript" that includes all grades for all classes, and indicates the date the student officially graduated.

For senior year classes, the class title and credit value are included on the transcript as usual. For instance, write, "American Literature and Composition: 1 credit".

Obviously, you cannot use the senior year classes to calculate the GPA, because grades aren't complete. Only count completed junior year classes for the GPA. When you send the transcripts at the beginning of senior year, include all senior year classes your child is taking on the transcript. Don't forget to include dual enrollment classes!

Complete the FAFSA

Fall is also when you will complete the Free Application for Federal Student Aid (FAFSA.ed.gov). The FAFSA will determine how much financial aid you may receive from the federal government (not from the college). You can start filling out FAFSA forms online on October 1st of senior year.

Develop the new habit of filling out the FAFSA every October from now on. You will start completing the FAFSA when your eldest is a senior in high school and continue filling it out every year on October 1st until your youngest exits college. The FAFSA needs to be filled out for every year you want to receive financial aid from the federal government in college.

Financial assistance from the federal government is given out on a first come first served basis. You want to be first in line for the money! Don't procrastinate!

The FAFSA will calculate your Expected Family Contribution (EFC). The EFC is what the federal government thinks your family can afford for college. Unfortunately, it is usually a laughably large amount!

If you end up with two or more children in college at any given time, the EFC calculation doesn't change. In other words, you are expected to contribute the same total amount regardless of how many children are in school. With two kids in college it's like getting a 2-for-1 deal! If you as a parent attend college at the same time as your child, then you're still getting the 2-for-1 deal for your EFC calculation and resulting funds from the government.

Even before October 1st, you can prepare for the FAFSA. Request your FSA ID for the FAFSA at studentaid.ed.gov/sa. You need an FSA ID for yourself as the parent, as well as for your student.

You will need your previous year's tax information handy to fill out the FAFSA.

It is possible to estimate the amount of financial aid you may expect to receive from the federal government in advance. See FAFSA.ed.gov/FAFSA/app/f4cForm for an online estimate. Keep in mind that far more financial aid will come from colleges than will come from the federal government through the FAFSA form. While the FAFSA is important and every penny counts, focus elsewhere to get the big scholarships!

Chapter 3

Winter of Senior Year

The winter of senior year is when homeschooling gets a bit more intense. Hopefully your applications are already completed and mailed! Now the focus has shifted to academics and getting school work done. But there are other jobs to do as well.

College Interviews

During winter of senior year, you may start hearing back from colleges. It's not uncommon to hear from colleges in December or January, or sometimes even as late as March. A college may indicate they liked your child's application and extend an invitation for a college interview. If you've already visited the college, they may not ask for a separate interview. Sometimes a college will consider your prior college visit in lieu of an interview.

Some colleges require interviews. Other colleges require interviews of certain student groups, such as homeschoolers. Sometimes the interview is required as part of a scholarship competition. These interviews can be very important and worth a lot of scholarship money. If your child attends an interview, they might have a chance to earn a bigger scholarship!

Go for a visit when a college requests it. While at the college, encourage your child to act assertive and confident. This can be remarkably difficult for some children! Even children who think quite highly of themselves can have trouble being assertive and confident in a high-pressure situation. Practicing at home in advance can help because one of the skills colleges look at is social skills. While homeschoolers generally have great social skills, not all colleges know this. The interview is a chance to for your child to demonstrate their exceptional social skills.

Make sure your child is well rested for the college interview. Sometimes this is the most neglected part of being prepared. Your child will be more pleasant, more confident, and more assertive when they've had enough sleep!

Have your child practice a firm handshake before the interview. Remind them to make direct eye contact, and to speak clearly. Your child will be doing all the talking. Parents shouldn't be present at the interview.

Have your child dress conservatively and act professionally. Explain to your children what the word "act" means; they don't have to be professional, they only have to pretend to be a professional. They are "acting" professional.

Remind your teen to turn off all electronics during the interview. Setting gadgets to vibrate or turning down the volume isn't enough. They still will distract your teen. All electronics should be turned off completely. The interviewer will know if your teen isn't paying full attention to them, or is texting in their pocket using one hand!

Let your child know that none of the questions they will be asked are supposed to be answered with a "yes" or "no." There also won't be right or wrong answers. The interviewer always wants your child to elaborate on the answer. Questions are meant to lead your child to speak in response. They need to provide specific details in each answer to their interviewer.

Interviewing skills learned through college interviews can also be useful for job interviews and career fairs. These are great skills and will stick with your child for the rest of their life. For more information on how to win a scholarship competition and ace an admission interview, see Appendix 2.

Plan the Celebration

Start planning the graduation celebration in the month of January. Sit down with your child and ask them what they would like to do for their senior party. Whether you have a party all your own as a family or celebrate graduation with a group, you will want to make plans for senior portraits. Professional photographers fill up quickly with graduates, so make an appointment for senior portraits in January, or even earlier.

If you are joining in a homeschool group graduation ceremony, registration forms are often filled out in January. You will also need to order a cap and gown, whether it's a group or private affair. Most kids will be eager to don the cap and gown – it's a big deal – a meaningful tradition.

Remember to order graduation announcements. If you want to make them yourself, give yourself enough time to design, print, and decorate. Consider having them printed out at a copy center for a professional touch.

You can order an elegant diploma from www.HomeschoolDiploma.com. They have wonderful supplies for graduation. I also have some diploma templates available on my website for my Gold Care Club members if you decide to print something up yourself instead.

I encourage you to hand a diploma to your child in a celebratory way, even if you don't have a formal ceremony or party. Being handed that high school diploma is a rite of passage. When they apply for a job and are asked if they have a high school diploma, you want them to reply without hesitation that they do. High school graduation is a big deal and it's time to celebrate!

For more information on planning a great graduation, check out my book, *Graduate Your Homeschooler in Style* on Amazon.

Chapter 4

Spring of Senior Year

Springtime! The applications are finished and the end is in sight. What a relief! Now you and your student can start to think about other things.

Save Money on College

You can save money on college tuition. Seek private scholarships based on your child's special abilities or essays your child has written. These scholarships are offered by private corporations rather than from the federal government or colleges.

You should be able to find scholarships designed just for residents of the state where you live. Many of these scholarships are not based on the family's financial need, so earning scholarships is possible even if you aren't a low-income family. Do an internet search for your state name and the word "scholarship" to find scholarship possibilities in your own state.

To find more scholarships, you can also register with more than one scholarship matching website, such as Fastweb.com. Follow the three "F's" when applying for college scholarships: find, filter, and follow through. Find appropriate scholarship opportunities by filling in the student profile carefully. Filter through all the scholarship options effectively, so you don't waste time applying for scholarships your child isn't qualified for. Then make sure you follow through with the applications together with your teen.

Waves of Scholarships

The financial stress of a parent with a college-bound child is much more extreme during the spring of senior year. You know your child is going to college because they've been admitted to several, but you don't have a clue how you're going to pay for any of them. Don't lose heart! Scholarships come in waves. They don't all come in when your child gains admission, but they will arrive gradually throughout the year.

The first wave of scholarships is based on GPA and SAT or ACT score. These first scholarships offered are usually for large amounts, perhaps $8,000 or $10,000 per year for each individual college. This sounds fantastic until you put the amount into context. College costs can still leave you with $20,000 to $50,000 a year or more to shell out, which can be a bit scary.

The second wave of scholarships can come from either colleges or the government, or both. These scholarships are based on financial need as determined by the FAFSA information you provided in October. They are need based scholarships, based on income. The government will let you know how much money they are going to chip in or loan you for your child's education. Even if the federal government judges you not eligible for a scholarship, colleges can still see your FAFSA information and understand your student has a financial need. Many colleges will offer much more financial aid to low-income families. You might be surprised by what colleges consider low income, though. Even if your family earns a good income, colleges may still offer financial aid.

The third wave of scholarships is the money colleges offer because of your child's college application as a whole. This money may be based on special merit or skill. It may be offered due to a stellar interview, success in a scholarship competition, or because your child has won the National Merit Scholarship (through the PSAT/NMSQT).

You may hear your child has gained admission to a college in December and continue to wonder how to pay for college until early January, when you find out your child will be receiving an award because of their SAT scores and GPA. At the end of January, you may find out your family will be receiving scholarship money from the federal government. By

May, you may finally find out the total you will need to pay for college. It can feel like a long time between December and May, and the wait can cause stress.

During this time, remind yourself that scholarships come in waves and just wait patiently for the next wave. Don't panic, just keep swimming! While waiting, apply for private scholarships and don't give up hope.

Making a Choice

Spring is when you and your child will need to make the big decision—which college to attend. Rejoice as the news comes in with each admission and scholarship offer. Then compare the offers your child has been given.

When you sit down together to make a choice about which college you can afford, ignore the scholarship amounts and focus on your bottom line. How much will each college cost you out of pocket? Because each college has different tuition fees and costs involved, the only way to compare them is to determine how much money you have to pay out of your own wallet.

As you make the college choice, you will want to consider the post-graduation employment rate of each college. Only 60% of students are employed upon graduation at some colleges. That's not a good bet if you or your child must go into debt to attend. If your college choice has a 95% employment rate, then it's much more likely your child will be employed upon graduation.

Whoever is shelling out the money gets to make the ultimate decision. Most often, it's the parent's money that's being shelled out. Even if your child wants to go to a specific college, you're their financial source. When you are looking at colleges, consider the programs available, the out-of-pocket cost, the employment rate upon graduation, as well as where the student desires to go.

The National Candidates Reply Date is May 1st. Every student across the nation must decide where they will be attending college on or before May 1st. Once you've decided, there are fees you have to pay as soon as you accept the admission offer. You will also be set up with a payment plan schedule.

If you feel like your child is just not ready for college, you might encourage a gap year. Taking a year off before college can give your child the opportunity to mature before they go. Do your research first and talk to your college of choice regarding how they feel about deferrals. Your child can apply for college, earn admittance and scholarships, and ask for it all to be deferred for a year.

Asking for More Money

Think about how you're going to afford college tuition and related costs. How much debt are you willing to take on, if any? How much should your child end up with, if any?

It's always best to try to avoid debt. Hopefully you have done your research on how to get those big scholarships early in the high school years and have set yourself up for the very best scholarships.

However, some debt might be reasonable. College does have value and adults with college degrees get better paying jobs. Financial advisors will tell you that although you generally don't want to go into debt for anything, debt incurred for a mortgage or for a college education are considered "good" debt.

How do you decide what is a reasonable debt load? Imagine your child graduates from college and all they can find is a minimum wage job, working full time and living at home. How much could they pay off in one year? That would be a reasonable amount of debt.

It is possible to ask for more scholarship money. You can try to negotiate with the college for a reasonable debt load. This is one of the reasons why it's helpful to apply to four to eight colleges, regardless of your situation. Then you can tell your first choice college that your child can't afford to go to their school and another college is offering your child $5,000 more a year. Ask if they can match that amount since you prefer their school. It's a bit like negotiating your salary for a job.

You can also ask for more money after the National Candidates Reply Date. After that date, there is scholarship money that was set aside for students who have since decided not to attend, and this money is once again available! There are no guarantees, but it is a good opportunity to ask.

Another good time of year to ask for more money is after the school year begins, for the same reason. Some students may not show up at the dorm in September, because they haven't been able to come up with all the money required. If they don't attend the college after all, any scholarship money they were promised is now available for someone else.

When you ask for more money, obviously threats and bribery won't work. Something else that won't work is expressing an entitlement attitude. The "I'm a homeschooler and you're discriminating against me by not giving my child a scholarship" or "My child should be able to go to college for free" or "My friend got into your college and isn't paying as much" kind of attitude is not going to work – simply be very polite and kind as you ask for more money.

Chapter 5

Summer After Senior Year

After senior year is complete and all of your child's academic work is finished, you must send in their transcript to the college with final grades. Usually these are mailed in June. Include your child's graduation date on the transcript, which can simply be stated as "June of 20xx". The transcript doesn't have to include the exact date and time of your graduation ceremony.

Once you have sent the transcript to the college your child is going to attend, you can focus on some gaps in your child's life skills. Make sure they know how to do their laundry. They will also need to know how to do a reasonable amount of cooking and cleaning. In college dorms, students may be put on a cleaning rotation and have to take turns cleaning the toilets, the sinks, and/or the showers.

Make sure your child is set up with a bank account and a credit card or debit card. You as parents should also have some way of transferring money into your child's bank account. If they need money for books or whatnot, you want to be able to get it to them right away. Mailing a check is not the best option—the mail can take quite a while and your child could even forget to check the mailbox! There are online options for sending money—look into them in advance.

Shopping for College Life

If you haven't already, now is the time for you and your child to shop for what they will need in their new life at college. If your child will be living in a dorm, try to contact their roommates in advance. This way, you can ensure there won't be two mini-refrigerators crowding the dorm room!

Also be sure to check college policies, especially regarding anything that generates heat or uses electricity. Your child may not be able to keep it otherwise! At the college my children attended, mini-refrigerators had to be a certain size, for instance.

Girls may want to contact their roommate in advance so they can coordinate room colors. Sometimes they will simply split the room with different colors or patterns. For boys, it might be helpful to try to get them to at least agree on a single solid color, like navy blue or brown.

You can also start helping your child pack for college. They are going to need:

- bedding
- a computer or tablet
- school supplies
- cooking and eating supplies—usually there is a microwave available in the dorm
- cleaning supplies
- flip-flops to cut back on athlete's foot

- toiletries and a bucket of some sort to carry them to the bathroom
- laundry supplies
- storage for documents such as their driver's license, records, and bank account information where they can keep important papers out of the way and confidential

If you start thinking about these purchases early in the year, then you can use this list for purchasing birthday presents, Christmas presents, Valentine's Day presents, and goodies for the Easter basket. Also check for any items the college itself has suggested. If you want a more complete college packing list, check out my article at:

HomeHighSchoolHelp.com/college-packing-list

Chapter 6

Fall After Senior Year

Children Become Adults

After senior year, your child's transition to adulthood will become more noticeable. This is a very emotional time for parents, and often for children as well. Parents need to expect great changes in children as they become adults. Try to keep in mind your five-year plan. In five years, you want to have a healthy, happy, and close extended family. Focus on that and don't sweat the small stuff.

When your child is in college, don't treat them like an eight-year old anymore. Think of them as a young adult and try to maintain a healthy relationship so you'll be a close family five years from now.

The most difficult thing about having a child in college is knowing when and how to step in. If your child does something life-threateningly stupid, you should intervene. Involvement with drugs and driving under the influence, for example, are serious concerns requiring immediate parental involvement.

Another time to step in and intervene is when your child is engaging in something life-alteringly stupid. If they are posting inappropriate things on social media for instance, you need to talk to them. It's not a private environment and it may affect their post-graduation prospects because future employers may see what's posted.

There are other times when you don't step in, and instead allow your child a chance to learn real life skills and deal with consequences of their choices. I realized I was an adult when I was in college and there was a spider on my wall. I screamed and smashed it on the wall. A week later, the spider was still a mess on the wall and I kept wondering why the spider didn't disappear as it always had at home. That was when I realized I had to clean it up myself! Your child will have to face natural consequences in college, such as what happens when they use up all of their money too quickly.

Enjoy Success

Enjoy your success in the fall after senior year! Face the empty nest eagerly rather than with regret. When your children are in college, you can go back to caring for your house and for yourself the way you did before you were busy homeschooling.

When your children are in high school, begin to make a list of things you want to do after they graduate. You may want to spend time doing volunteer work, or pursue any number of your own interests!

It took me a while to adapt to the changes. Our lives have changed since our children graduated. We go out to dinner more. You will be amazed how much easier it is to afford dinners out when you don't take your children with you – especially boys who eat buckets full! We go out to nice restaurants and I make special meals at home more often – I even buy steak!

Change doesn't have to be a bad thing.

The Empty Nest

You may experience intense feelings when you face an empty nest. Tears, feelings of loss, and sometimes feelings of hopelessness are common. On the flip side, there may be extreme joy and relief! If you're a mom, this is often complicated by raging hormones that women our age may experience right around the time of high school graduation. These hormones can make things seem so much worse.

The pain of facing your new empty nest can take time to heal. I encourage you to give yourself plenty of time. Eventually you will find a new normal and come to acceptance. Look forward to your child's visit for Thanksgiving or Christmas to help cope.

Toward the end of homeschooling, you start to wonder about the next stage of life. What will you do when you aren't homeschooling? I can suggest what *not* to do. I saw a woman at the store who was talking about how bored she was with her life. She had attended *four* Weight Watchers meetings during the week, not because she was overweight, but because she was *bored*! Although I'm a big fan of Weight Watchers, I wondered about her experience. Is that all there is to life after children?

When it's your turn, don't be bored! Instead, give yourself away! Help other parents homeschool. Become a board member for your state homeschool group. Volunteer at a local food or clothing bank. Give yourself away in new ways, too! There is nothing that can take your mind off your own problems more than helping people with even bigger troubles!

Develop a Bucket List

What have you always wished you had time to do? When I was homeschooling, so many times I had to say "No" to fun things. I had kids at home, I had to get dinner on the table, and there were 12 soccer practices to attend each week! When the kids are gone, it is your time to say "Yes!" to fun things you have put off!

If you are ending your homeschool career soon, start making a list! List all the things you wish you could have done over the past few years, because your turn is coming soon. Make a list of volunteer positions that sound like fun. Make a list of homeschool organizations you would like to help. Make a list of fun ways you would like to serve your community and your church.

After years of serving your family, soon it will be your turn to take care of yourself. This list will be invaluable during those first few too-quiet days.

Stay in Touch

Stay in touch with your child in meaningful ways. Make sure your teen knows they are loved and cherished, not for their performance in college, but for who they are. You want to shower them with love, but in moderation. Remember they are learning to be adults. Let them be independent. Don't be over the top – no phoning, texting, or messaging them all the time!

Social media is a wonderful communication tool, because you can see what your teen is up to without contacting them too much. You can see they're alive and well and some of what they're doing. Be careful you don't post so much that you make your young adult uncomfortable though.

Send gifts that will help them realize they're still loved and cared for. Sometimes college kids get sad at Thanksgiving if they don't get to come home, or on Valentine's Day, or other holidays. Sending goodies can help them get over these hurdles. Prayer also helps!

Plan some visits in advance, either to visit them or for them to come home. It can help your teen feel settled when they know they can at least come home for a weekend or week to decompress. When they do come home, they may not be talkative. They may simply want to be at home, back the way it was for a while, before going out to face adulthood again.

Chapter 7

When Bad Things Happen

Bad things can happen, even to good homeschool families. As Robert Burns said, "The best laid plans of mice and men often go astray."

When you start homeschooling, you don't plan on having a health crisis or family trauma, but bad things can happen. We are not immune to difficulty simply because our children are counting on us. Sometimes the best you can do is to throw the ball toward the end zone and hope someone catches it. Sometimes you need to pray for a touchdown.

To prevent major upheaval, work conscientiously on your homeschool each year. When things are going well, cover the core subjects each year, right from the beginning of high school. Try to avoid dropping classes unless it is a true emergency. By planning ahead like this, nothing will ever deter you in your homeschooling success.

I want to share with you an important story about success, perseverance, and planning ahead in case of a crisis year. This is the success story of Brittany, a 20-year-old woman. Here is what she wrote (used with permission).

Problem without Regrets

"Dear Mrs. Binz,

I happened upon your website today and I'm hoping you can help me. I'm not sure I'm your traditional candidate, or that my situation is common. But you seem like someone who knows a lot about homeschooling and I'm hoping you can give me some advice. My name is Brittany. I'm 20 years old and I was homeschooled by my mother starting in the second grade. I was homeschooled through the rest of elementary school, middle school and through most of my senior year. Here's where things get complicated.

In my senior year my grandmother became very ill and I was greatly needed to help care for her, so for all practical purposes I dropped out of school to do so. I kept saying I'd start back, but my grandmother stayed sick for over a year and a half and things just didn't work out for me. I do not regret taking care of her though. I just wanted to make that clear, because I don't want to sound like I begrudge that time away from school. Family took precedence over school. I knew I'd have my entire life for school.

So last year I was going to finish what I had left of high school and start pursuing college, like I've always dreamed of. But then family health tragedy struck even closer to home. My mother had a massive stroke and has suffered severe effects from that. Her ability to speak is very limited and her mobility was also altered. She is now wheelchair bound. Right now I am her primary care giver, so obviously I still haven't completed what I have left of high school. But enough back story, I know you're probably busy, so here are my questions/problems.

I have no transcripts. My mother, God bless her, did not make them, so I'm doing my very best to assemble them now. Do I fill them out through the part of my senior year where I had to stop and then submit them that way along with my college applications when I'm ready to start applying? I don't want to lose those credits, because I was a very good student. I took a lot of electives and things that I'd really like for colleges to see. So how do I do that?

My plan was to get my GED this month or the next, take the SAT in March, register at the local community college for the summer semester, and then transfer to Western Michigan University (if they'll have me) as an art major. (Yes, I realize these are lofty goals. haha)

I know this is a long email and that my situation is really complicated, but please if you have any advice or tips for me, I'd greatly appreciate them. Because I'm simply lost right now and I hoped you might be able to guide me.

Sincerely,
Brittany"

A Compelling Advantage

I really enjoyed consulting with Brittany. I told her she had one real advantage: a *compelling* personal story. Colleges love to provide admission and scholarships to students with unusual life situations, who have overcome obstacles. A compelling admission essay, transcripts, and SAT should be able to help her achieve her dreams. Brittany purchased my Total Transcript Solution and a Gold Care Club membership and we began talking on the phone for consultations.

It soon became obvious that Brittany was anything but a drop out. She was well-spoken, well-educated, and an excellent writer. Her parents must have worked conscientiously with her during her early high school years. Working together, her transcript looked remarkably complete for a young girl with a complicated family situation. Though much of her transcript was completed by junior year, it was quite thorough.

We talked about how she could apply to a university immediately, rather than attending a community college first. This alternative plan could bring more scholarship money as she would be considered a freshman. Her original plan included obtaining a GED, but I thought that might not be necessary.

I suggested she pursue both options – college admission now and community college as a backup plan, in case the money didn't come through. Once we started discussing her homeschool classes, we realized she had enough credits to graduate, and enough to get admitted to college. There is a skill to pursuing both options at the same time. For college admission, the SAT is more important. I suggested she take this test as soon as possible. It's easy to delay the GED if necessary, because it's usually not a college admission requirement for homeschoolers.

During January, I explained how to proceed:

> "Your best chance of admission will happen if you apply as soon as possible (this week). Get your SAT or ACT scores in as quickly as possible, next time they offer the test. Write the application essay using the tips I gave you. In a few months, you will find out the admission and scholarship results. If you aren't happy with the scholarships, then go back to your original plan. If you *do* decide to apply to colleges, as soon as you have hit 'submit' on your application, you will need to fill out the FAFSA (fafsa.ed.gov). Filling out the FAFSA is a lot like federal income tax forms, but for college scholarships, and much of the financial aid money will come from

that form."

Her immediate plan was to work on her application essay for the college she wanted to attend. I advised her:

> "The strategy is like a 'Hail Mary' in football. You're just throwing the ball up once, just to see if someone catches it. We're hoping your application will be caught. If it's not, you have a good, solid back up plan. While I don't think you should cram, I do think if you take one sample test of the ACT or SAT at home, it could help. Try to get a letter of recommendation from someone who is well educated. A pastor, Mom's doctor, or other homeschool parents you know who are professionals. See if they could write it."

Brittany's high school education included plenty of English and history. She had completed Algebra 2 and Geometry, plus two years of Latin, before the family crisis occurred. Together, we were able to find 30 credits for her transcript, demonstrating her interests in delight-directed learning during her family trauma. In February, she found out she was admitted!

The two-pronged approach can solve the biggest fear some parents have, "What if I fail?" What happens if you *do* fail? You can try the Hail Mary Play, and apply for college anyway.

Failing in your homeschool can look significantly better than failing in public school. Without the "F's" and rock-bottom GPA, colleges may see a well-educated child with a willingness to learn. Reading, writing, and a work ethic can compensate for a lot.

Create a New Beginning

I was thrilled to hear the final report from Brittany. Success!

"Dear Lee,

I just wanted to email you and say I GOT INTO WESTERN MICHIGAN!! I literally just found out. I don't have my financial aid packet yet or anything, but I do know for sure that I got accepted. Thank you so much for all your help with everything so far. Now all I can do is hope for the loans, grants, and scholarships I need and I'm golden. So yeah, thank you so much for everything. Without all of your help, I would be nowhere near where I am right now.

Sincerely,
Brittany"

I explained she was receiving the first wave of scholarships within a week or two of application, because they are based on SAT or ACT scores. I told her, "Keep your Plan B in your back pocket, but also remember that scholarships come in waves, and you haven't even received the first wave yet." (See Chapter 4)

In April, she was still working hard on the details of financial aid. She asked me how to find more scholarships and I suggested my scholarship class. I told her to consider herself a high school senior or a college freshman. Since she had been notified she was admitted, she could say she was enrolled in college. I said:

> "If you can do this right away, and follow through during the summer, you could do pretty well. Also, speak to the college about your concerns. They may have additional scholarships at the college you can apply to as well."

Successful Result

In June, Brittany provided a follow up report.

> "Hi, Lee.
>
> I hope you're doing well. It's been quite a while since I've talked to you. Everything is still a go for attending Western in the fall. I got $15,000 in aid and scholarships, I'm going to get a student loan for the remaining $20,000 for my degree. $20,000 was my goal, so I'm more than happy with it and I'm still waiting to hear back on a few private scholarships. I'm just getting my student loan set up and

saving money at this point. I'm going to be taking Math, English, Art, French and possibly Sociology if the course load isn't too heavy. My moving date is August 27th. It'll be here in no time.

But anyway, I just wanted to thank you for all of your help with everything. Without you, there is NO WAY I'd be where I am right now. I'm so thankful I found your website. I think YOU are awesome and thank you again. God bless you.

Sincerely,
Brittany"

Take-away Lesson

This story is a lesson in encouragement. From the beginning, we could see how Brittany's family did things right. They educated their daughter, creating a strong, independent young woman capable of learning, reading, writing, and thinking. She didn't shirk academics during the beginning of high school, but pressed forward until stymied by trauma.

The lesson of this story is also a purposeful warning for homeschool families. I want homeschoolers to plan for a possible crisis year. I don't want you to assume something bad is going to happen, of course. But by planning for your crisis year, nothing will ever deter you in your homeschooling success.

Here is how to plan around a crisis year. Plan your high school courses for success. Make sure you cover all subjects (especially challenging ones) from the beginning – don't wait for senior year! Above all, keep your transcript and course descriptions up to date every year. Be prepared by staying on top of your homeschool responsibilities.

Chapter 8

The Panic Plan

The moral of Brittany's story is to try your best to avoid panic during senior year. As Brittany's story shows though, sometimes panic can find us! The bad news is there are many legitimate situations where you may feel panic during this critical year. The good news is that with proper preparation, these situations can usually be avoided. If panic is a reality or at least a real possibility for you, here are some brief tips to help you navigate back to calmer waters.

Plan Ahead

Make sure you plan ahead. It's difficult to complete college applications and everything that goes along with them quickly, so give yourself a lot of time. Pick up college applications in advance. Colleges will often waive the application fees if you ask for the application forms during your college visits. It can also help to complete some scholarship essays during junior year, to practice and to earn some private scholarships.

Twelve Step Panic Checklist

I have an emergency plan for families who haven't started preparing for the admission process prior to senior year. Here is a quick checklist for those panicky parents. When you recognize you are behind in senior year, immediately begin these steps.

1. Drop all homeschool work and activities and work on college applications instead.
2. Together, watch "Getting the Big Scholarships" and "Finding a College" (at HomeHighSchoolHelp.com).
3. Locate a college fair, put it on the calendar, and commit to going.
4. Register for the next available SAT

or ACT (if not already taken) and put it on the calendar.

5. Determine if you have all the classes colleges require.
6. Drop unnecessary classes and replace them with any missing college preparation classes.
7. Take the SAT or ACT (if not taken junior year).
8. Apply to at least two public and two private universities (include reach, fit, and safety colleges).
9. Write applications and essays, as required.
10. Complete the transcript as soon as possible. You can find help for emergency transcript preparation at www.TotalTranscriptSolution.com.
11. Turn in applications as soon as possible, transcript and test scores can follow, but must arrive by the deadline.
12. Return to your regular academic work.

No matter what stage of senior year you are in, and no matter how freaked out you are, concentrate on calmly working on the steps together with your child for hours each day, until everything is all filled out and turned in!

Suggested Reading

My book, *The HomeScholar Guide to College Admission and Scholarships* is a must-read. It can help you plan through the whole college admission and scholarship process. You can read about it here:

HomeHighSchoolHelp.com/
CollegeAdmissionBook

Another book you may find helpful is my Coffee Break Book, *Graduate Your Homeschooler in Style*, which will help you plan for your child's graduation and beyond, including a memorable graduation ceremony! Find all my Coffee Break Books on my Amazon author's page:

amazon.com/author/leebinz

I've included a summary of everything you need to know about college applications in Appendix 1, "Fifteen Point College Application Checklist."

Appendix 1

Fifteen Point College Application Checklist

I know parents are busy, sometimes too busy to even read a brief book like this. If this is you, I have summarized the major ideas about applying to colleges in this appendix. If you do nothing else, please read this appendix. It will also be a great thing for you to review periodically throughout senior year.

The goal of senior year is completing college applications. The difficulty is that applying to college is a "process" and not a "moment." Applications are not difficult, but they are very time consuming. Each university will have a unique process, unique forms, and unique requirements. It's complicated but not difficult. Use this simple checklist to make sure you aren't missing any pieces.

1. Start Early

First of all, you want to apply early and often. This means you need to hit the ground running. Begin filling out your college applications on the very first day of senior year. It takes effort, so you don't want to get into a time crunch.

If your child will be in dual enrollment, it can help to start college applications in the summer prior to senior year. If they will be taking college classes full time, they won't have the energy to complete applications as well. Colleges often provide admission and scholarships on a "first come, first served" basis, so applying early is important.

2. Application Essays

College applications require multiple self-reflective, technically perfect essays. Homeschool parents understand that "technically perfect" is difficult. It takes lots of time, editing, and rewriting. Other people need to read it and give feedback or suggestions. For teens, "self-reflective" is equally difficult. It often takes a long time to even consider what a self-reflective essay might be. Make sure you plan for plenty of time for the "considering" stage of writing. If you do begin filling out applications on the first day of senior year, you can put your other English curriculum aside for a while. Decide you are doing a unit study on essay writing during September.

3. Review the Forms

Colleges can also have some complex application forms. These forms include many questions.

Applications will also require letters of recommendation for your student. It's difficult to decide who should write recommendations. The recommender must have plenty of time to write the recommendation. Once written, allow some time for it to be mailed to the college.

4. Understand Deadlines

In some ways, filling out college applications feels similar to filling out your federal tax forms. Firm deadlines, high expectations, fine print, words you don't understand, and if you mess up, there's a huge financial consequence in the end. Oh joy! Plan ahead and spend time on it, making sure you start the first day of senior year. Even if it's due in the last week of November, you'll still need plenty of time to get it ready.

5. Complete your Transcript

Senior year is the absolutely critical time for you to complete high school records. You will need to turn in your child's transcript when you turn in the application. To do so, include the classes your child is currently taking. If they're taking Pre-Calculus this year, then you put Pre-Calculus on the transcript. But instead of a final grade, you can say To Be Determined (TBD) or In Progress/In Process (IP) to show they are currently taking this class and will be finished in June. Have your transcript ready to go with their application early in the fall during senior year.

6. Prepare a Reading List and Course Descriptions

Most colleges ask for additional material beyond the transcript. So, create a reading list including books read for school and pleasure. I strongly suggest parents write course descriptions as well. These are most important for selective colleges, when the student has a strong college preference, or if good scholarships are critical. However, all applications may be strengthened by course descriptions, so I always recommend preparing them "just in case." Include a paragraph of what you did, a list of what you used, and an explanation of how you graded.

7. Complete Homeschool Records

Additional homeschool records may be required. A university could ask for samples of work from any class, and sometimes request these samples in the student's handwriting. They may request an activity and award list, or resume.

Some applications may ask for a statement from the homeschool parent, or require a counselor letter that is completed by the parent. It's sometimes helpful to write a cover letter as an introduction to your transcript. Since there are a variety of things that may be requested, planning ahead will give you the time you need to complete everything required.

8. Repeat Tests

The second priority during senior year is to shore up any shortcomings from junior year tests. Repeat the SAT or ACT if the scores were poor and could be improved, or if the test was missed. If your child needs to take these tests in senior year, register for the first testing opportunity so the results are promptly available. If subject tests are needed, you want to find out right away and register for these tests as well.

9. Fill Gaps

Look over a list of recommended courses, and try to discover any major educational gaps. It can happen! "Oh my goodness! I have completely forgotten economics!" Small gaps, such as a semester economics course, can be quickly filled when discovered early. Major gaps, such as lack of foreign language, may need to be filled with community college.

For example, foreign languages may be required by a choice college. Taking foreign language at a community college for one year can provide two or three high school foreign language credits to fill this gap. Community college is not something I normally recommend, but it can help fill major gaps discovered during senior year.

10. Watch the Calendar

Watch deadlines and details and mark them on your calendar. Colleges can have unusual requirements and can ask for some strange things. Be sure you give them everything they need and want. If they ask for a lab write up from your high school biology class, submit it. If they want a transcript in a signed envelope, prepare it that way. Find out and give them the details they want.

11. Complete the FAFSA Application

The FAFSA is used to determine how much money the government believes you as parents can afford to pay for college. Complete the FAFSA on October 1st of senior year. Financial aid is first-come, first-served. Believe me, you want to be first!

12. Anticipate Scholarship Results

Expect three waves of scholarships. When your child applies for college, they're given some immediate scholarships based on SAT, ACT and GPA. The second wave of scholarships is based on the FAFSA and financial need. That third wave of scholarships is based on merit or other factors. The third wave of scholarships may not arrive until May or June, and may even arrive during summer.

For this reason, the most difficult time for parents is the time between March and June. This is when parents know where the child wants to attend, but they have absolutely no clue on how to pay for it. It can be a challenging and stressful time. I encourage you to be patient until you get the final wave of scholarships somewhere between March and June.

13. Brace for Changes

It's important to remember you're going to experience dramatic changes over the four years of high school. Maturity happens. The changes you saw in your child between newborn and four years old are similar in scope to the dramatic changes that will occur between freshman year and senior year. Don't be afraid your child won't ever be mature enough to graduate, or they'll never go off on their own. Huge changes take place between freshman and senior year so don't give up hope. Expect dramatic changes so you're prepared for anything.

14. Be Prepared

Teenagers do change their minds and they may go back and forth between, "I'm going to college," and, "I'm never going to college. What a stupid idea." Situations can change. You want to plan ahead as much as you can possibly can so if your situation changes either for better or for worse, you'll be prepared. Be prepared in case your teenager balks at tasks required during senior year. Senior year is very close to adulthood, and sometimes adults don't want to do what their mothers tell them to do. Be prepared when teenagers make adult decisions as they are becoming adults. Also avoid fear that immobilizes you.

15. Start Early

The best success comes to those who work the process early. Hit the ground running. The first day of senior year is the day you get to start working on applications so you can get them turned in as soon as possible. I understand that in reality, not everyone will plan ahead.

Appendix 2

How to Win a Scholarship Competition and Ace an Admission Interview

You've done a great job educating your kid. They are bright, intelligent, well socialized and have an area of passionate interest. All the required classes are under their belt, with great grades, excellent test scores, and wonderful letters of recommendation. You have kept complete and accurate homeschool records. This means your child might be invited to a scholarship competition. They could be invited to interview at a prestigious school.

A college may want a thirty-minute interview for admission, or an eight-hour competition for scholarships. How do you prepare for something like this?

Do the Ground Work

During an on-site scholarship competition, colleges are looking for students with great social skills. Does the student look them in the eye and have a firm handshake? Can they talk with anyone of any age? Are they polite, yet confident? One of the reasons homeschoolers do so well in these competitions is because they often have these skills! So, relax—most of your preparation for the competition has already been done!

Schools are looking for someone who's warm and friendly. They understand kids will sound like kids and not like adults. At the same time, they are trying to decide if "the lights are on" inside. For example, if they mention a current cultural issue, can the student give an educated opinion?

Colleges are looking for an investment. They want to give money to someone who is going to improve the college's bottom line. This means they are looking for students who will stay at their college for all four years, and graduate with a good GPA. They want students who will succeed in graduate school or career and students involved on campus, who are leaders among peers.

Homeschoolers do have an advantage. We have a curriculum advantage, with the ability to choose appropriate curriculum to educate our children. We have the testing advantage, by allowing our children to take tests that highlight their academic strengths. We have the comprehensive record advantage, by providing explanations of what we taught. And we have the character advantage, because we have time to shape and mold our children's character and behavior every day.

These are great advantages. But when it's time for your children to interview or compete for scholarships, knowing you have the advantage isn't enough. This is when you need lists!

Plan Ahead

As in a job interview, colleges will likely ask your child, "Tell me something about yourself?" For this reason, it is a good idea to brainstorm some possible answers with your student beforehand. Colleges may ask specific questions about a student's area of specialization. Think for a moment about possible topics and stories your student could mention.

Help your child also think of questions they could ask the college about their major, or the on campus living situation. Bring anything they ask you to. Take along the music if your child is performing. Bring a portfolio if the art school asks for it. Read every bit of material they send, looking for a list of things to bring.

Here's a list of important questions and ideas for your student to review before the interview:

Twelve Ways to Prepare Your Thoughts

1. Accept the offer to interview or compete as soon as possible.

2. Review your comprehensive homeschool records together with your parent.

3. Think about questions you want to ask the college.

4. Make a list of things you want to be sure to say about yourself.

5. Review the essay you submitted with your application.

6. Consider any special situation or transcript grade you need to explain.

7. Be ready to describe ways you can make the college stronger.

8. Consider living on campus.

9. Commit to graduating in 4 years.

10. Commit to earning a good GPA.

11. Think about how you will be active on campus.

12. Have goals for after college.

Thirteen Practice Questions

1. Why are you interested in this college?

2. What will you contribute to our college community?

3. What high school courses have you enjoyed the most?

4. What is the most important thing you've learned in high school?

5. How do you define "success?"

6. What are your strengths? Weaknesses?

7. What activities do you enjoy the most?

8. How would you describe your biggest achievement?

9. What is the hardest thing you have ever done?

10. What is your opinion on (insert current event here)?

11. If you could talk to one person (living or dead) who would it be and why?

12. How do you spend your summer?

13. What do you expect to be doing 5 years from now?

Six Helpful Be-Attitudes

1. Be genuine—who you are, not pretending to be someone else, or stretching the truth.

2. Be engaged—pay attention to the person speaking to you.

3. Be assertive—everyone is in the same boat, so demonstrate confidence.

4. Be interested—ask questions about

the college, programs, and activities.

5. Be polite—dress conservatively and speak politely to everyone while on campus.

6. Be thankful—write a thank you note, and send by email and snail mail.

Fourteen "Don't Do" Tips

1. Don't look at the clock or your watch.

2. Don't look at your phone—turn it completely off and leave it off.

3. Don't be late.

4. Don't be arrogant or boast.

5. Don't lie, because they can figure it out.

6. Don't respond with only yes or no answers.

7. Don't tell the school they are not

your first choice.

8. Don't memorize a prepared speech.

9. Don't ask questions covered by the college catalog.

10. Don't chew gum.

11. Don't wear cologne or perfume.

12. Don't swear or use too much slang.

13. Don't be rude to the receptionist or staff.

14. Don't bring a parent into the interview.

Relax and breathe deeply. You have been well prepared for this moment. Think about a few ideas you can use for the general "who are you" questions. Think of it not as a competition so much as an opportunity to meet some great new friends and share your opinions on a wide range of topics. You *can* do this! Simply let your light shine and have fun!

Scholarship Competitions

My kids experienced this process when they went to an all-day competition for a full-tuition scholarship at Seattle Pacific University. SPU invited 108 of the top applicants to compete, and 10 were chosen. Two of the kids selected that day were homeschoolers—and both were my children! Boy, did we have a party!

When my children were invited to the competition, they were asked to bring something that represented them. My younger son brought a charcoal drawing he had made of the French Economist, Jean Baptiste Say. My older son brought the chess demonstration board he used to teach chess in inner city classrooms.

Every applicant displayed fabulous academics, with great test scores, and an interesting passion. All were able to talk intelligently. There were some "Survivor" moments, when students would try to out-answer, out-talk, and out-volunteer others. My younger son was surprised that other kids spoke up more than he did!

I remember when they came home from the competition, "I don't know if I won, but I had a great time! All the kids were so nice!" They *loved* getting to know new people—smart kids with many interests. They met kids who talked about interesting things all day, and had a blast!

Ultimately, we learned that our students weren't chosen solely on their performance that day. They were also chosen for intangible reasons. How did they interact with other students? How did they handle the competitiveness? How did they behave when they thought nobody was looking?

Selection boiled down to socialization and character. Talk about a homeschooling advantage! Ultimately, I think they won because of how much fun they had. They went in with the right attitude and their authenticity and enthusiasm were apparent to all. Even my "quiet" son did well, thus proving it's not as much about being outgoing as it is about being genuine.

Karla's Experience

Karla did a wonderful job of preparing her son for a scholarship competition, and has some fabulous advice!

"Lee,

I wanted to share my son's scholarship interview and experience, but it was too long to put as a Facebook post. I hope you don't mind hearing the longer version! My son, Jeremy, has been accepted at George Fox for the fall and plans to go into the electrical/computer engineering program. His SAT scores were such that he has already received the $10,000 scholarship. In addition, he was invited to their scholarship competition in February.

On the way to the college his dad and I spent a fair amount of time discussing what we thought they might ask in an interview: 'Tell us about yourself. What are your strengths and weaknesses? What are your goals?' etc. Several ideas came straight from your post about these interviews.

After the interview, I grilled him on what he had been asked. He said they asked about steward leadership, which was the topic of the application essay. Then the professor asked, 'I see that your GPA was 3.97. Why wasn't it a 4.0?' Boy, we hadn't anticipated that one! So, Jeremy replied that it was his freshman biology class, explaining that he and biology just didn't get along. Then the professor said, in an amused voice, 'Wait, it says you are homeschooled! Your mama gave you a B!!??' Jeremy said, 'Well, yes, I guess I deserved it.' And the professor added, 'We homeschool, too, and we did that to our son once.'

We were quite amused by that, but secretly I was wondering if that lower grade would be a detriment since all the others probably had 4.0s, or if that would work in his favor since it showed he and his mom are honest.

Last week he got an email with the results of the competition. Guess what—he won! He will receive, in addition to the SAT scholarship, a scholarship for engineering, the highest for this competition. He also won a vocal scholarship as a non-music major.

There's our story. Thought you might enjoy it, especially the comment about "mama giving a B." Have a great day—and thanks for listening!"

~ Karla in Washington

This is a great story from Karla, and it points out how human and humorous admissions folks can be. Karla's story has some great advice. Plan ahead for interviews. Practice questions with your child. Don't give up hope!

Give Thanks

If there was ever an instance that called for a heartfelt thank you note, it is after a scholarship competition. Have your child say thanks by email and snail mail and include specific details about their visit. Below is an example from my son, Alex.

Notice the specific compliments to the university, the professor of the class attended, the interviewer, and to the other students.

"Dear Mike,

Thank you so much for both the scholarship competition and our interview on Monday. The competition in general was exceptionally well-organized for the candidates. The group discussion was excellent, fast-paced and quite insightful. I also thoroughly enjoyed my visit at the Capstone: Political Economy class, taught by Lisa Surdyk. It was fascinating to listen and participate as the class worked their way through current political issues using economic principles.

I also wanted to thank you for our interview and time together. You may not realize it, but the questions you asked, and even the visual feedback, really helped as I was formulating my thoughts. This was my first experience in an interview where I was able to talk about my motivation—not just what I'm passionate about, but also why. The beauty in fine arts is generally understood, but I am equally fascinated by the aesthetic of society and nature. I want to thank you for asking great questions.

Good luck in choosing the finalists from the exceptional candidates I met yesterday; you have quite a job ahead of you!"

Sincerely,
Alex

Be sure your child thanks the college for the interview or scholarship opportunity. Decisions may not be made for weeks, so this is their last opportunity to leave a positive impression. A thank you note provides a wonderful conclusion to a great opportunity.

Good luck!

Afterword

Who is Lee Binz, and What Can She Do for Me?

Number one best-selling homeschool author, Lee Binz is The HomeScholar. Her mission is "helping parents homeschool high school." Lee and her husband, Matt, homeschooled their two boys, Kevin and Alex, from elementary through high school.

Upon graduation, both boys received four-year, full tuition scholarships from their first choice university. This enables Lee to pursue her dream job—helping parents homeschool their children through high school.

On The HomeScholar website, you will find great products for creating homeschool transcripts and comprehensive records to help you amaze and impress colleges.

Find out why Andrew Pudewa, Director at Institute for Excellence in Writing says: "Lee Binz knows how to navigate this often confusing and frustrating labyrinth better than anyone."

You can find Lee online at:

HomeHighSchoolHelp.com

If this book has been helpful, could you please take a minute to write us a quick review on Amazon?

Thank you!

Testimonial

Dear Lee,

My kids have graduated high school and are both now in college. I've put off canceling my subscription because I couldn't stand to part with another friend. However, it is past time for me to say farewell and move on. I can't thank you enough for all your advice and support during the high school years. You were an answer to prayer. Everything we encountered during these four years of high school, you've addressed in way one way or another.

I'm not sure I ever told you the story of how God led me to you, so I will share that story now. In February of my daughter's junior year of high school, I began to get serious about putting her transcript together. Friends had provided examples of a high-level transcript showing course name, grade, and credit earned. However, I felt that this high-level listing just did not reveal how much effort went into our studies and outside activities. So, as I've always done throughout our homeschooling years when faced with a problem, I presented my dilemma to God. After approximately two weeks in prayer over this situation, I came upon your website. I knew from deep within my soul it was an answer to my prayer.

I subscribed to your e-mail blog and became a Gold Care Club member. After I took your webinar, "Making a Transcript" I was off and running. Your easy style replaced my fear with empowerment. You and I used some of the same books in science (Apologia) and math (Saxon) and allowing me to use your templates minimized my learning curve. I am a very detailed person so your templates meshed with my detailed style.

I looked forward to reading your daily e-mail blogs. I continued to take your webinar classes and I used your consultation services. All total, it took me six months to finish my daughter's transcript complete with course descriptions, reading lists, activity and awards lists, student work samples and letters of recommendation, and even a profile letter.

Every single page highlighted her talent. For example, she chose to include her favorite Scripture on the inside front cover across from the Table of Contents page. In addition, although I did not give her a credit for art, I did include one of her black and white drawings on the inside back cover and a color drawing on the outside back cover page.

I have to admit, writing course descriptions was a bigger job than I anticipated but with your continued encouragement I knew I could push through and finish. Her transcript was ready by September 1st of her senior year in high school.

Now it was time to start writing our son's course descriptions; his was much easier to write because the format was already in place. For many of his courses, all I had to do was input his grades. As you would say, "easy, peasy!"

In conclusion, I have to say that the finished product of the transcript and course descriptions really is something to see. When looking through the bound book, it is obvious we were serious about our academics. It also gives a detailed account of the high school years for each student, which is even better than a year book. But more importantly, it attaches high value to my students which are also my children. It sublimely tells them they are important. In its own unique way it says, "I love you." Both of my student-kids not only understand that message, but thanked me for it.

Lee you have been such a blessing to me. I thank my God every time I remember you. Philippians 1:3

In all sincerity,

Christine

For more information about the **Gold Care Club**, go to: www.GoldCareClub.com

Also From
The HomeScholar...

- The HomeScholar Guide to College Admission and Scholarships: Homeschool Secrets to Getting Ready, Getting In and Getting Paid (Book and Kindle Book)
- Setting the Records Straight—How to Craft Homeschool Transcripts and Course Descriptions for College Admission and Scholarships (Book and Kindle Book)
- TechnoLogic: How to Set Logical Technology Boundaries and Stop the Zombie Apocalypse
- Finding the Faith to Homeschool High School
- The Easy Truth About Homeschool Transcripts (Kindle Book)

- Parent Training A la Carte (Online Training)
- Total Transcript Solution (Online Training, Tools and Templates)
- Comprehensive Record Solution (Online Training, Tools and Templates)
- Gold Care Club (Comprehensive Online Support and Training)
- Silver Training Club (Online Training)

The HomeScholar Coffee Break Books Released or Coming Soon on Kindle and Paperback:

- Delight Directed Learning: Guiding Your Homeschooler Toward Passionate Learning
- Creating Transcripts for Your Unique Child: Help Your Homeschool Graduate Stand Out from the Crowd
- Beyond Academics: Preparation for College and for Life
- Planning High School Courses: Charting the Course Toward High School Graduation

- Graduate Your Homeschooler in Style: Make Your Homeschool Graduation Memorable
- Keys to High School Success: Get Your Homeschool High School Started Right!
- Getting the Most Out of Your Homeschool This Summer: Learning just for the Fun of it!
- Finding a College: A Homeschooler's Guide to Finding a Perfect Fit
- College Scholarships for High School Credit: Learn and Earn With This Two-for-One Strategy!
- College Admission Policies Demystified: Understanding Homeschool Requirements for Getting In
- A Higher Calling: Homeschooling High School for Harried Husbands (by Matt Binz, Mr. HomeScholar)
- Gifted Education Strategies for Every Child: Homeschool Secrets for Success
- College Application Essays: A Primer for Parents
- Creating Homeschool Balance: Find Harmony Between Type A and Type Zzz...

- Homeschooling the Holidays: Sanity Saving Strategies and Gift Giving Ideas
- Your Goals this Year: A Year by Year Guide to Homeschooling High School
- Making the Grades: A Grouch-Free Guide to Homeschool Grading
- High School Testing: Knowledge That Saves Money
- Getting the BIG Scholarships: Learn Expert Secrets for Winning College Cash!
- Easy English for Simple Homeschooling: How to Teach, Assess and Document High School English
- Scheduling—The Secret to Homeschool Sanity: Plan You Way Back to Mental Health
- Junior Year is the Key to High School Success: How to Unlock the Gate to Graduation and Beyond
- Upper Echelon Education: How to Gain Admission to Elite Universities
- How to Homeschool College: Save Time, Reduce Stress and Eliminate Debt

- Homeschool Curriculum That's Effective and Fun: Avoid the Crummy Curriculum Hall of Shame!
- Comprehensive Homeschool Records: Put Your Best Foot Forward to Win College Admission and Scholarships
- Options After High School: Steps to Success for College or Career
- How to Homeschool 9th and 10th Grade: Simple Steps for Starting Strong!
- Senior Year Step-by-Step: Simple Instructions for Busy Homeschool Parents
- How to Homeschool Independently: Do-it-Yourself Secrets to Rekindle the Love of Learning
- High School Math The Easy Way: Simple Strategies for Homeschool Parents in Over Their Heads
- Homeschooling Middle School with Powerful Purpose: How to Successfully Navigate 6th through 8th Grade
- Simple Science for Homeschooling High School: Because Teaching Science isn't Rocket Science!

Would you like to be notified when we offer the next *Coffee Break Books* for FREE during our Kindle promotion days? If so, leave your name and email below and we will send you a reminder.

HomeHighSchoolHelp.com/
freekindlebook

Visit my Amazon Author Page!

amazon.com/author/leebinz